WHY DO TIGERS HAVE STRIPES?

Mike Unwin

Designed by Sharon Bennett

Illustrated by Robert Morton, Steven Kirk, Gillian Miller, Robert Gillmor, Treve Tamblin and Stuart Trotter

Editor: Helen Edom

Science consultant: Dr Margaret Rostron

CONTENTS

Additional designs by Non Figg

A world of colors

Many animals, such as tigers, have interesting colors or patterns. This book explains how colors and patterns help all kinds of animal, from the biggest elephants to the tiniest insects.

A tiger has a striped pattern. Can you think of any other animals with stripes?

Matching colors

Different animals' colors often match the places where they live. The oryx is an antelope that lives in the desert. Its pale color matches the sandy background.

In deserts there are few places to hide from enemies. Sandy animals are hard to spot because they blend in. Colors or patterns that help animals to hide are called camouflage.

An oryx is pale and sandy like the desert.

These desert animals have sandy-colored camouflage to help them hide from hunters such as hawks and foxes.

Scorpion

Gerbil

Hidden hunters

Most animals run away if they see a hunter coming. Camouflage helps hunters to hide so they can catch other animals to eat.

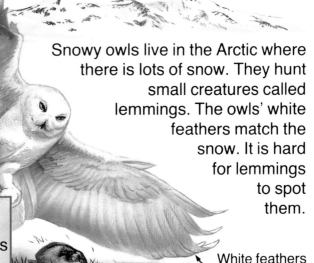

Snowy owls live in the Arctic where there is lots of snow. They hunt small creatures called lemmings. The owls' white feathers match the snow. It is hard for lemmings to spot them.

White feathers blend in with the snow and sky.

Lemmings

Forest greens

Many animals that live in rainforests are green to match the colors of the leaves. This camouflage makes them very hard to see.

Look at the green tree frog in this picture. How many other animals can you spot?

Tree frog

Blue waters

Camouflage is also important under the sea. Many sharks and other fish are colored blue or grey. This helps them to blend in with the colors underwater.

Blue sharks

3

Patterns

Background colors are not the only kind of camouflage. Patterns also help animals to hide.

Breaking up shapes

A tiger in the zoo looks big, bright and easy to see. But in the forests and long grass where it hunts, a tiger can be hard to spot.

A tiger's stripes seem to break up its shape into small pieces. It is hard to see among the patterns and shadows of the background. This helps it to creep up on deer and other animals.

Seeing in black and white

This black and white picture shows how a leopard looks to an antelope.

Many animals such as antelope cannot see colors. They see in black and white. This makes it very hard for them to make out an animal, such as a leopard, whose pattern breaks up its shape.

Lying in wait

The gaboon viper is a snake that lives on the ground in African forests. Its complicated pattern makes its shape hard to see against the leaves.

Small animals cannot see a gaboon viper lying in wait for them. When they get close, the viper kills them with a bite from its poisonous fangs.

From a distance

The ringed plover lives on beaches. Close up its markings look bright. But from a distance you can only see a pattern that looks like the pebbles.

If the plover keeps still, it seems to disappear into the stony background. Enemies cannot spot it unless they are close.

Ringed plover

Seaweed shapes

The sargassum fish has strange lumps of skin that stick out from its body. These make its shape hard to see. It seems to disappear among the seaweed where it lives.

People hiding

Soldiers wear uniforms with special patterns. This helps them to blend into the background, just like tigers do.

5

Shadows and light

Light and shadow can make animals stand out from their background.

Lying flat

This bird is called a stone curlew. It is well camouflaged, but you can still see its shadow. In daylight, solid things always have shadows. This helps you to see where they are.

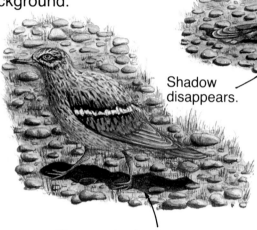

Shadow disappears.

A stone curlew lies flat on the ground so it looks small. This makes its shadow disappear so it is even harder for enemies to spot.

Stone curlew's shadow.

Flat shapes

Some animals have flattened bodies. Enemies do not notice them because they leave hardly any shadow.

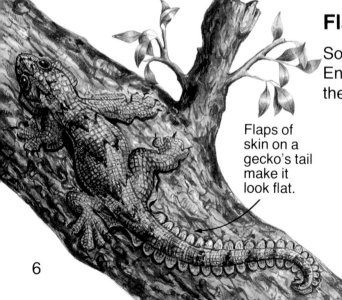

Flaps of skin on a gecko's tail make it look flat.

The flying gecko is a lizard that lives on tree trunks. It has a flat body with flaps of skin that press down on the bark. This helps it to hide.

Dark and pale

You can often spot solid things by seeing the light shining on them.

Sunlight makes the top of this rock look lighter than the background.

No sunlight reaches the bottom, so it looks darker than the background.

The impala, like many animals, is colored dark above and pale below. This is the opposite of the natural light and shadow that fall on its body. It makes the impala harder to pick out from its background.

From below

Many water birds such as puffins are white underneath. They swim on the surface of the water and dive down to catch fish.

From underwater the surface looks bright because of sunlight above it. It is hard for fish to spot puffins from below. Their white undersides are hidden against the bright surface of the water.

Hiding with mirrors

Many sea fish such as herrings have shiny silver scales on their sides and bellies. Underwater, these scales work like mirrors. They reflect the colors of the water, so the fish become almost invisible.

7

Disguises

Some animals are shaped to look like other things. This helps them to hide. These insects all have disguises that help them hide in forests.

This caterpillar looks just like a bird dropping, so nothing wants to eat it.

The thorn bug looks just like a thorn on a branch.

The leaf butterfly's folded wings look like a leaf on the forest floor.

The stick insect looks just like twigs.

Standing straight

Animals can help their disguises to work by the way they behave. The tawny frogmouth is a bird with colors like bark. If it is in danger, it points its beak upward so it looks like a dead branch.

Deadly flowers

The flower mantis is a hunting insect. Its body is the same color and shape as the flowers where it hides.

Other insects that visit the flower do not notice the mantis lying in wait to catch them.

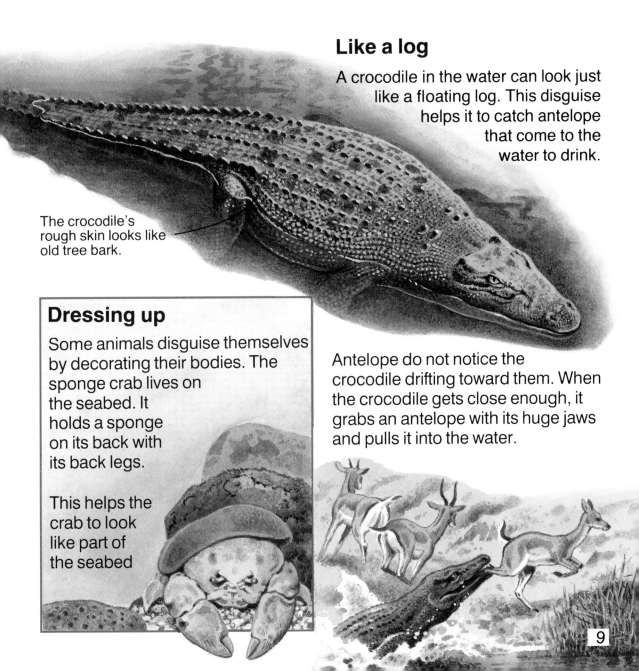

Like a log

A crocodile in the water can look just like a floating log. This disguise helps it to catch antelope that come to the water to drink.

The crocodile's rough skin looks like old tree bark.

Dressing up

Some animals disguise themselves by decorating their bodies. The sponge crab lives on the seabed. It holds a sponge on its back with its back legs.

This helps the crab to look like part of the seabed

Antelope do not notice the crocodile drifting toward them. When the crocodile gets close enough, it grabs an antelope with its huge jaws and pulls it into the water.

Surprises

Some animals stop enemies from attacking by tricking or surprising them. They often use colors or patterns to help.

Frightening eyes

Many hunters are frightened if they suddenly see a big pair of eyes.

This swallowtail caterpillar has patterns that look like eyes. Birds think they belong to a bigger, more dangerous creature, so they leave the caterpillar alone.

The caterpillar's real eyes are hidden under here.

A bright flash

The red underwing moth looks well camouflaged on bark. But if it is spotted by a bird, it opens its top wings to show the bright red underneath.

Bark

A sudden flash of red surprises the bird. It leaves the moth alone.

Missing the target

This hairstreak butterfly has a pattern on its wings that looks like another head. Birds peck at the wings by mistake. This gives the butterfly time to escape.

Head pattern

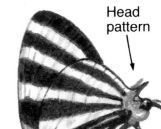

The real head is at this end.

Puffing up

Some animals make themselves look bigger to trick enemies. A long-eared owl spreads its wings and puffs up its feathers to frighten enemies away.

This owl looks twice as big as usual.

Playing dead

Some hunters, such as hawks, only attack living creatures. An opossum is a small animal that pretends to be dead when it is in danger. When the danger has gone, the opossum gets up again.

An opossum pretends to be dead by rolling over with its mouth open.

Looking both ways

In India tigers sometimes attack farmers. Tigers are scared by people's faces so they attack from behind. Farmers wear masks on the backs of their heads to scare tigers away.

11

Keep-away colors

Some animals do not try to hide. They have bright colors and patterns that are meant to be seen. These colors are a warning to their enemies.

Remembering colors

Black and yellow patterns are easy for animals to remember. Wasps are bright yellow and black. They can give their enemies a painful sting.

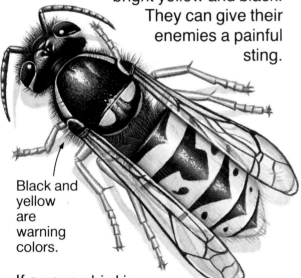

Black and yellow are warning colors.

If a young bird is stung by a wasp, it remembers its pattern. It will not try to catch a wasp again, because it knows that black and yellow things hurt.

Eating bees

A few birds, such as bee-eaters, have found a way to eat bees safely. They are not put off by warning colors. Bee-eaters bang a bee on a branch so its stinger is squeezed out and broken.

Being seen

Many poisonous animals do not run away. Instead they show off their warning colors to their enemies.

The deadly poisonous arrow-poison frog does not hop away from enemies like other frogs do. It crawls around slowly to show off its colors.

Fierce black and white

The ratel is an African badger. Its white back makes it easy to see. Although it is quite small, it is very fierce and is not afraid of any other animal.

The ratel has strong teeth and claws.

The ratel does not need to keep a look-out for danger like most animals do. Its colors warn enemies that it is too dangerous to attack.

Smelly warning

Skunks are small animals with a bold pattern. They can squirt a nasty, smelly liquid at enemies such as dogs.

A spotted skunk stands up on its front legs to show its pattern. This warns the dog to stay back. If the dog comes closer, the skunk sprays it.

Signals for people

People use warning colors just like animals do. Red often means "hot", "stop" or "danger".

This red tap warns you to be careful because the water is hot.

13

Copying colors

Some animals survive because they have colors and patterns that help them to look like other kinds of animal.

Coral snake

Poisonous or safe?

Can you tell the difference between these two snakes? The coral snake is very poisonous. Its bright colors are a warning.

The king snake looks like a coral snake, but it is not poisonous at all. If you look hard you can see that its pattern is slightly different.

King snake

Other animals are afraid to attack the king snake because it looks like a poisonous coral snake.

Which is the wasp?

Some insects look just like wasps though they do not have stingers. Most animals do not attack these insects because their colors remind them of stinging wasps.

Can you guess which insect is a wasp? Look on page 24 for the answer.

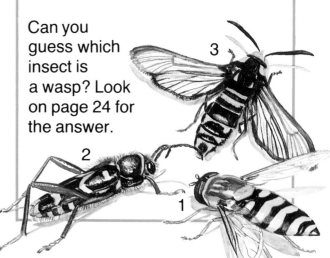

Ant antics

Most animals leave ants alone because they bite and sting. Some kinds of spiders look and behave like ants to fool their enemies.

Ants

The spider holds up two of its eight legs so it appears to have only six legs, like an ant.

The spider's upright front legs look like an ant's feelers.

Getting close

The cleaner fish helps bigger fish by cleaning unwanted dirt and lice from their skin.

Cleaner fish

The saber-toothed blenny looks like a cleaner fish, but it is really a hunter that tricks other fish.

Saber-toothed blenny

Big fish let the blenny come near because they think it is a cleaner fish. But the blenny attacks them and takes bites out of their fins.

Whose egg?

Can you tell which of these eggs doesn't belong?

Reed warbler

The middle one is a cuckoo's egg. The rest belong to the reed warbler.

The cuckoo lays its egg in a reed warbler's nest. It is the same color as the eggs that are already there. The warblers think the cuckoo's egg is their own so they look after it.

15

Signals

Some kinds of animals use colors and patterns as signals to each other.

Danger

A rabbit has a short, fluffy, white tail. If it sees an enemy such as a fox, it runs quickly back to its burrow, flashing its tail in the air.

The white tail is a signal to other rabbits. It says "danger!"

Follow my leader

Ring-tailed lemurs are animals with long black and white tails. When a group of lemurs is on the move, they hold their tails up like flags.

Lemurs' tails help them to see each other and stay together. They are signals that say "follow me".

Getting angry

A tiger has bold, white spots on its ears. If one tiger is angry with another, it turns its ears back to show the white spots.

The white spots are a signal that warns other tigers to keep away.

Looking different

Colors can make it easier to tell similar animals apart. This helps animals to recognize others of their own kind.

Goldfinch

Chaffinch

These are the wings of two different finches. Their shape and size are the same, but the patterns and colors help to tell them apart.

Being fed

Baby birds in nests wait for their parents to bring food. The babies' mouths are brightly colored inside.

These baby great tits have bright orange mouths.

When a parent arrives with food, the babies open their mouths wide to show the color inside. This is a signal to the parent. It says "feed me!"

People's colors

People also use colors to tell each other apart. All sports teams wear their own colors. This stops them getting mixed up with each other.

Different colored shirts help two soccer teams to tell each other apart.

Mysterious lights

Hatchet fish live deep at the bottom of the sea, where it is very dark. They have small patches on their bodies that light up and flash on and off.

Scientists think these lights could be signals to help hatchet fish recognize each other.

Showing off

Many male animals have bright colors to make them look attractive to females. This helps to bring the male and female together to breed.

Bright or brown

Male and female birds often look different from each other.

A male golden pheasant has beautifully colored feathers which he shows off to attract a female.

The female pheasant has much duller colors. This helps her to hide when she is protecting her eggs and chicks.

Risky colors

Bright colors can also attract enemies. In spring a male paradise whydah's bright colors are easy to spot, and his long tail makes it hard for him to fly away.

After the whydah has found a female he loses his colors and long tail. For the rest of the year he stays plain brown.

Putting on a show

Some male birds put on a show to attract females. Every spring, male ruffs gather together. They puff up their feathers and fight. Females choose the males that put on the best show.

Three different male ruffs fighting.

18

Colorful lizards

A male anolis lizard has an orange flap of skin under this throat. Usually it is folded up. But sometimes the lizard puffs it out and nods his head to show off the color.

The bright throat attracts females. It also warns other males to keep out of the area.

Fierce faces

Mandrills are African monkeys. A male mandrill has a colorful face that gets brighter when he is looking for a female. The biggest and fiercest males are brightest of all.

A female mandrill chooses the male with the brightest colors. Other males keep away from him.

Collecting color

A male bowerbird attracts a female by building a pile of twigs called a bower. He then decorates it with shells, flowers and bright, shiny things.

A female bowerbird chooses the male with the best bower. She then builds a nest and lays the eggs.

19

Making colors

Fur, feathers, scales and skin can be all sorts of different colors. Animals get these colors in many different ways.

Colors from food

Flamingo's feathers are pink because of a coloring called carotene which is found in water plants. Flamingos get carotene by eating tiny water animals that feed on these plants.

Often flamingos in zoos are not as pink as wild ones, because there is not enough carotene in their food.

Shiny colors

Many birds, such as sunbirds, have bright, shiny feathers. These change color when light falls on them from different directions.

This sunbird's feathers change from blue to green as the light shines on them.

Killed for colors

Some snakes are becoming rare because people kill them for their beautiful skins.

This bag is made from the skin of a python.

Growing green

Animals do not normally grow green fur. But this sloth looks green. This is because tiny green plants called algae grow in its fur.

Jigsaw

Butterflies' patterns are made by thousands of tiny different-colored scales that fit together.

Peacock butterfly scales

This is how the wing of a peacock butterfly looks close up. Can you see how the scales are arranged in rows?

Black fur

Animals have a kind of coloring in their bodies called melanin. Melanin makes dark colors in fur and skin.

A black panther is really a leopard born with more melanin than usual. Its fur is black. But if you look closely you can still see its spots.

White all over

Sometimes animals are born white. They have no melanin so they cannot make dark colors. These are called albino animals.

An albino blackbird has white feathers.

Changes

Some animals can change their colors. Chameleons are lizards that change the color of their skin to match different backgrounds.

This chameleon has a green pattern when it is hiding among leaves.

On sandy ground the same chameleon turns brown. It is always very hard to spot.

Sole survivor

The sole is a flatfish. It hides from enemies by lying flat on the sea bed. Its color depends on where it lies.

This sole is the color and pattern of the pebbles on which it is lying. If it moves onto sand, it becomes sandy-colored.

Sudden changes

If an octopus is in danger, different colors flash over its body. This surprises enemies and gives the octopus time to escape.

Colors also show how an octopus feels. For example, an angry octopus often turns red.

White for winter

Many animals that live in cold parts of the world turn white in winter. At the end of summer an Arctic fox sheds its brown fur and grows a white coat.

Fox in summer   Fox in winter

White fur helps the fox to hide during winter when the ground is covered in snow. In spring the fox's brown fur grows back again.

After the fire

In Africa, fires often change the color of grassland by burning it black. Some kinds of grasshopper can turn from green to black to match the color of the ground.

Before the fire the grasshoppers were green like this one.

Colors of the land

The color of an African elephant's skin can change, depending on the soil where it lives. This is because it covers itself in dirt and mud to cool down.

This elephant lives in a place with red soil, so it has reddish skin.

Index

Insect answers

Page 14 – None of the insects in the picture is really a wasp. Number 1 is a fly, number 2 is a beetle and number 3 is a moth. You can see a real wasp on page 12.

This edition first published in 2006 by Usborne Publishing Ltd., Usborne House, 83-85 Saffron Hill, London EC1N 8RT, England. www.usborne.com